Children of the Air

T0161319

Children of the Air

Theodore Deppe

Alice James Books
Cambridge, Massachusetts
1990

Library of Congress Cataloging-in-Publication Data
Deppe, Theodore, 1950-
Children of the Air. I. Title
PS3554.E625C47 1990
811'.54   89-24409
ISBN 0-914086-91-X

Cover and book design by Anna M. Pulaski.
Illustrations by Rachel Pulaski.
Cover photograph of the 1938 Hurricane by William H. Foley,
courtesy of the *Providence Journal.*
Typesetting by The Writer's Center, Bethesda, Maryland.
Printed in the United States of America by Evans Printing Company, Concord,
New Hampshire.

Publication of this book was made possible with support from the Massachusetts
Council on the Arts and Humanities, a state agency whose funds are recommended
by the Governor and appropriated by the State Legislature.

Alice James Books are published by the Alice James Poetry Cooperative, Inc.

Alice James Books
33 Richdale Avenue
Cambridge, MA 02140

Acknowledgments

Grateful acknowledgment is made to the following publications
in which versions of some of these poems first appeared:

Andrew Mountain Press Broadside Series: "Thallium Scan"
Beloit Poetry Journal: "Altenbrücken," "The Gatekeeper"
Cincinnati Poetry Review: "Three Letters from Wolf Creek"
Contemporary Review: "Loyalties to What We Know"
Crazyhorse: "Breaking and Entering," "Les Enfants du
    Paradis"
Cumberland Poetry Review: "Counting the Stations"
Greenfield Review: "Game Near Ocotal"
Kansas Quarterly: "The Crucifixion of the Apostle Peter"
Louisville Review: "Hurricane's Edge," "March Thaw"
Negative Capability: "Richmond Avenue"
Peregrine: "Student Art Therapist," "Chandeliers in
    the Desert"
Red Fox Review: "The Garden of Last Things"
Southern Poetry Review: "The Garden of Saint Dymphna"
Wind: "Riding with the Prophet"
Worcester Review: "Houses in Cézanne," "Immigrant
    Wife," "Prophet for the New Year"
Yarrow: "Sarah"

Some of these poems appeared in a chapbook, *Necessary Journeys*,
published by Andrew Mountain Press, 1988.

Appreciation is acknowledged for an individual artist grant from
the Connecticut Commission on the Arts.

For Annie

Contents

Part One

March Thaw   *11*
Three Places in New England   *13*
Les Enfants du Paradis   *16*
Thallium Scan   *18*
The Chaperone   *19*
Garden of Last Things   *20*
Children of the Air   *21*
Richmond Avenue   *22*
Blue Grass   *24*
Counting the Stations   *26*
Riding with the Prophet   *28*
The Gatekeeper   *29*

Part Two

Three Letters from Wolf Creek   *33*
Greenbrier   *35*
West Branch   *37*
Sarah   *38*
Dante   *39*
Student Art Therapist   *40*
Crucifixion of the Apostle Peter   *41*
Loyalties to What We Know   *42*
Prophet of the New Year   *44*
Garden of Saint Dymphna   *46*

Part Three

Annus Mirabilis   *51*
Breaking and Entering   *53*
Immigrant Wife   *55*
The Blasket Clearances   *56*
Houses in Cézanne   *58*
Altenbrücken   *60*
Game Near Ocotal   *61*
Chandeliers in the Desert   *62*
Abington Four-Corners   *64*
Gloria   *67*
Hurricane's Edge   *68*

Part I

Part I

March Thaw

Say the two of you quarrel after lunch
    about the dishes. And since
the sun is out, let's say you both
    let the whole mess soak,

walk the dog to Mashamoquet Park.
    By the footbridge, you are startled
by two lovers, naked from their waists
    down. You turn away at first,

then watch,
    because they block your path,
because they're indiscreet
    and riveting. Oblivious to your gaze,

the woman is spread-eagled
    on a wool coat, pale arms
thrashing the matted grass, and the man,
    muscular and young, all thrust

and buttock and sun. But
    isn't there—in their imagined privacy—
something humorous,
    as your dog trots over the bridge

to make friends? Even
    when you call him back, they don't
look up. And yet this abandonment
    to legs and sun: admit it,

we envy them.   This first spring day
    they make the two of you choose
whether to turn home or walk
    over the bridge right past them.

Or else, undress each other
    on your own side of the brook,
mirror images of these lovers whom,
    like gods, you cannot disturb.

Three Places in New England

1

I'm afraid I said something inexcusable
to Putnam's librarian about her failure
to have a recording of Charles Ives'
Three Places in New England,
a work my brother says celebrates
this ailing mill town. "K-Mart
might have it," the librarian says,
"try the record department at K-Mart."

Down the street, the fire they finally
put out yesterday at the chemical plant
has started up again. A man guarding the roped-off area
tells me it may burn another three months.
Hot spots in the rubble keep igniting.
In the alley, two half-melted semis, like monuments.

2

I watch from the disappointing record section
as they inventory plastic flowers at K-Mart.
A heavy woman with a clipboard claims, "it's the worst
job in the store—I get it every year."
Down-aisle a woman with waves of black hair
counts the latest fashions in roses
with a man she calls Mark. Feigning interest

in artificial yucca plants, I listen as he swears
he'll never touch another "care-free flower."

She tucks a silk iris behind her ear.

A smoke-scented day of sirens, rumors, the sky
down the block like orange cellophane, crinkling again.
Twenty thousand artificial roses.
Her hand resting briefly on his shoulder as she talks.

3

It wasn't the town of Putnam
it turns out, it was Putnam's Camp,
south of Danbury, where the boy Charles Ives

waited for the July 4th parade.
From opposite directions, two local bands
entered town, each playing

a different march.   The boy was confused
and exhilarated—was this planned
or did somebody ball things up?—

the loud bands out of sync, each
lock-stepped into its own piece, two armies
approaching the town's only graveyard

and Ives—conducting both bands
uphill—springing to his feet

4

which leaves the town of Putnam
smoldering in January sleet,
without the music, the resonance I thought it had.

Imagine the silence of the town tonight,
the stillness after freezing rain
turns to slow dabs of snow, and Mark

from K-Mart climbs carefully the steps
of her apartment.   He can barely see the white
blur of the Quinebaug.   Since the town's water

is still contaminated, he brings champagne
and a dozen silk irises.
She lets him weave blue flags through her dark hair,

and all of this—for the moment—without sound,
music, or words.

Les Enfants du Paradis

Dreams, Baptiste claims, are the same as life
or else it's not worth living—good theatre,
dark prospects. In this film, interrupted
by world war, lovers play out their afternoon
on the Street of Many Murders where tightrope walkers
perform above dandies and thieves. The last show

before they demolish the Trans Lux, and the final image
of Part One is a worn velvet curtain falling slowly
over a long shot of Garance who's had to compromise
with love to stay alive. Years ago, I watched
the huge, shirred curtain descend at the Harris Grand.
To encourage good dreams, Mother took me

only to movies that ended well, love stories
or Disney. Once, I jogged in place as Walnut Street
funneled wind from Canada and Mother argued
with the ticket-seller who wouldn't open the doors
until 1 o'clock. Children bickered in the cold
while inside the "Napoleon of the Moment,"

as Mother called him, joked with the concessionaire
and a slow-motion fountain of popcorn rose
behind tinted glass. But then we're inside,
admiring walls that open like stage settings
onto balconies and turrets. The Trans Lux
is shabbier than the theatre from my childhood,

and even its closing, its free show
and sad banners, pales beside the night
I bicycled downtown to watch the Harris Grand burn,
the flames inside so I had to imagine them
as their roar intensified each time a fireman
entered the glass door.   I can't remember

names on the marquee—probably some 50's comedy,
Doris Day and Rock Hudson shriveling
in the projector.   I couldn't imagine
Bloomington without that theatre,
can't imagine losing the Trans Lux now
where we struggle after Garance in the festive crowd,

watch as she disappears,
then push after her until Baptiste too, is lost,
swallowed in a high angle shot of carnival,
a multitude of celebrating lovers
and none of it ending well, the revelry and songs
of extras on the Boulevard du Crime.

Thallium Scan

(for Voyd Turner)

The vivid shades of the scintillation camera
are not the colors of our world: the heart's
failing pump reflected in molten tones
that spell a passing, a brilliant orange fist
opening and closing, over and over,
like a screen door slamming itself shut
in an empty farmhouse.   So that we think each time
the door swings open we should be able to see out—

and yet the scanner shows only the heart.
It is all mapped out, in thallium,
without the mansions, without the many
rooms or windy fields.   It misses
the canopy of fire raised all around us,
illuminating the darkness, where we live.

The Chaperone

Forgive me, just a day ago
you warned me to write
less about fire, but this morning
I chaperoned a trip to the art museum

and the bus filled with smoke.
In breezy rain I lifted
the children out the rear exit,
led them down the Interstate's

narrow shoulder.   Rescued
six at a time, we arrived
in small, wet groups
at the museum, and saw nothing

that rivaled the blaze
from that yellow bus
or the pillared smoke against
overcast skies.

I think we were happiest
standing in spring rain,
watching flames
fanned by sudden gusts.

The Garden of Last Things

(for Paul Ross Lynn)

This time of night,
        this time last year,
                you cut cosmos in your garden

surrounded by grandchildren
        who picked armfuls of zinnias
                before the first killing frost.

Held back so long
        they were like angels of apocalypse
                finally given permission

to pick anything that bloomed.
        The children stayed out late,
                there was a festival air,

they placed mason jars
        crammed with flowers
                in every window of your house.

You stood in the garden, your stroke-
        slowed voice faltering
                over words that might

hold them.   The children flew,
        like sparrows, to the porch
                calling as they went.

Children of the Air

Because all day my kids heard the canned calliope
from the nearby park, we're in the third row
gazing up at "The Children of the Air,"
two brothers and a sister from Mexico, performing

on the high-wire without nets.   The boys' arms
flare up at the end of each trick, their faces lit
with practiced smiles, but their sister, Alma,
cartwheels over their heads, arrives at safety

with a look of indifference, a distant, skinny girl
in black mesh stockings.   I'm too concerned
with their risk to enjoy the act, keep scanning
the crowd for our local doctor, and yet

when my children, walking home, ask what I liked
best, I say the aerialists.   We balance
on the sidewalk edge as though high above the ring
and when my daughter slips, I imagine how she'd vanish

from the spotlight as she fell.   She hops
back on the curb, wavers towards the streetlamp,
a pale double of the sequined girl who caught the light
this evening, who did a double flip

off one brother's shoulders, ran to the wire's end
and, whether it was weariness or disdain, barely
acknowledged our applause.   Maybe there's such a thing
as a habit of equilibrium, something learned

early by a girl who glitters in the light.
But now, alone in her trailer, does she wonder
how many years she'll keep this balance,
what she'll do when she knows it's gone?

Richmond Avenue

It's romantic, they decide, an apartment
so close to the tracks.   Their first place
off campus, and when they wake that night
to a train's whistle they roll closer together
on the single-bed mattress from his childhood,
start making love before the train's gone.

A few nights later, she starts charting the trains,
wants to be able to say, "There goes the old
two-thirty special."   She thinks there's a hint
of order in the times that night: 12:30, 2:30, 4:24.
He's not so sure.   They have classes in the morning,
evening jobs, so they content themselves with a nocturnal

record of train whistles in Richmond, Indiana.
The next night: 12:20, 3:10, 6:44.
He suggests the times are random,
a record of chaos in America's railroads.
When, after two weeks, she asks if he can see
a pattern, he says he thinks the numbers prove

they live too damn close to the tracks.
It turns out they fight a lot,
and when they make love
they do it for other reasons than the pulse
and moan of a train.   There might be another woman,
he can't seem to make up his mind.

But this is the way the railroads disappear.
Another fight, smoldering all morning,
until they stop talking and watch the arrival
of a storm—heavy rain and the scent
of early summer sidewalks.
They sit in the window, watching the downpour.

By nightfall the streets are flooded, the first
cool air in a week.   And by morning the rain's
still falling, a boy wades down Richmond Avenue
casting for trout, and they stay in bed—a day
without trains.   He caresses her lower back.
She proposes they graph the rain.

Blue Grass

I won't offer up this mass for the soul of Uncle Robert,
who hated Catholics and was buried in his Mason get-up—
but I thought of him after the drunk hunched up next to me
vomited on the floor during the creed.   Wiping his shoes
with his coat sleeves, he stopped and looked at me
the way Robert would have, eyes tightening,
said, "What the hell are you staring at?",
then staggered off, genuflecting
maybe two dozen times as he left the church.

So I stand during the intercessory prayers,
thinking how my uncle puked in a rusty bucket
while we drove him to the E.R.,
his pint of Jim Beam having failed to cure his chest pain.
He picked an awful night to die,
the same night the black cloud rose
from the Blue Grass Army Depot,
choking and panicking the families living downwind,
who arrived at the hospital certain the nerve gas

had finally leaked out.   We all knew it could happen,
the poisonous acid eat through its metal coffins,
seep from those crumbling bunkers, wipe clean
the eastern half of Kentucky.   Weeks later, we'd learn
they'd burnt tons of Agent Orange, but that night
the depot commander denied all knowledge,
blamed it on "student radicals."   He called back
every ten minutes or so, just to make sure
no one had died.   Each time the phone rang

Uncle Robert—strapped to his cot—called out
"Jerry! I know that's you. Come down here
and bust me out of this goddamned hole."
The black nurses kept giving him morphine,
hoping he'd sleep. I rise now for the consecration,
believing more in the senseless deaths
we're rushing toward than in anything else.
And later, in the parking lot, I look around
for the drunk, thinking

I know what he saw in my face to hate—not disgust,
he must have felt that himself—compassion, maybe,
thin as the scroll of ice I scrape from my windshield.
I don't insult my uncle with kind words or prayers.
He was a bastard: let him sleep.

Counting the Stations

(lines after the suicide of a favorite teacher)

We return for your funeral: a night
flight to Indianapolis, and then the long
car trip south through fog.   At my parents' house
I tuck my son into my old bed, a thousand
miles from his own.   "Close the closet door," he says.
I reassure him; he says, "You know what's in there.
Just close it!"   I do, and he lies back down.

Years ago, after your class, I drew a time-line
on this closet door.   The penciled names
rise out of the darkness now, like lights from the stations
of an underground.   Gauguin and Munch.   Goya
and Bosch.   They read like a litany of lost souls.
You taught us art by working backwards, leading us
past the donors and madonnas until at last we reached

Lascaux, and the caves of the ocher deer.   In that still
black light someone painted images against hunger and death.
You leaned against the blackboard and seemed to share
the gentle grace, the dreaming beauty of those deer.
But now I push back farther in those caves and find
the image of a wild boar, bristling with arrows, fighting
for its life, and losing.   Shrill and harsh and maddened

by pain, it thrashes in the dark.   It could bring us all
down.   It is the pig I thought we killed in childhood.
Father said slitting its throat would be too messy
so we shot it, six times because it wouldn't fall, each shot
searching for the small bright flame inside its brain.
Mother says you were out on bail, the phone kept ringing,
and you let it ring until the end, then shot yourself . . . .

I step outside, start on a walk, turn back
because a thought overtakes me at the hill's foot.
If I met you here, in this fog—if I walked with you
through this town we once shared, looked at the clapboard
homes, shrouded in mist, doorless—if I lived here still,
as you will, always—
I turn back because we've talked like this before
                                        and it doesn't end.

Riding with the Prophet

By the third night my father squints at the road
as if following faint deer tracks.
His hands shake at the wheel.   By now
I know I have failed him.   He won't say it
but I can hear his voice clearly: "Maps
of the outside world are nothing.
Look inside, are you listening to me?"

"No, I'm not," I think and keep on drawing.
I put down road numbers and schools, a heron
wading in the Little Wolf River, the name
of a waitress from the tag on her blouse.
But there are gaps in my map, times
I fell asleep and found he'd changed routes
again.   He liked unmarked roads best.

And at the map's center, the place where I woke
and heard the lull of his voice talking to itself.
My first glimpse of the desert: a sharp moon
above his shoulder, and the shapes
of dark mountains that traveled with us.
I wake now at a truck stop, someone tapping at the glass
and my father too tired to roll the window down

and order gas.   The pump-boy shrugs, swears,
walks away.   Farm trucks idle, unattended, exhaust
rising above the diner.   I close the door quietly, start
walking.   Time and again my father wakes
alone, follows my path through this red grass.
"There's going to be a new heaven," he says,
"and a new earth.   Be sure you get them on your map."

The Gatekeeper

Each year, returning home, I pass
the woman who sells quilts outside
Gnaw Bone, Indiana.   She sits in the shade
of a cottonwood, her work on the clothesline:
Rose of Sharon, Ladder to Heaven, Garden of Eden.

When I tell her she asks too little she says
they're just old scraps pieced together,
nothing special.   She offers me coffee,
sometimes corn bread.   But this evening
when Highway 46 straightens out before her house

I find her meadow crowded with people:
groups of women set out food, men
laugh together as their children play tag
in the dusk, the Quilt Woman
turns to face me,

and klansmen move through the gathering
in white robes and white hoods.
I slow the car to look, but young men
posted on the roadside idly raise their shotguns
and wave me on.   I take with me an image of home

they want me to see, though not clearly.
So now I have no home, or
have one and can no longer recognize it.
Or else have one that is bound
inextricably to evil, and still home.

Part II

Three Letters from Wolf Creek

1

We drink plum wine, walk the boundaries
of our land: juniper bushes and the black
fields of sky.   Sarah says she tries

not to be bitter, the treatments were just
storms like the ones that once rolled
across Oklahoma.   Curtains of fire

at every window.   Above Wolf Creek, memory enters
through the burning gate.   She sets up canvases
in every room, tries to salvage what she can.

2

Part of being her lover is trying to brush out
the black waves, trying to part her hair
with a key or a nail or a knife: the darkness

floods back in.   And yet her paintings
are always of light: cornfields radiant
under storm clouds, a waitress on break

staring out across the stippled river,
or the pineapple weed and sweet yarrow
that she's hung above our bed, suspended in sun.

3

The lights go out along Wolf Creek, the snows
erase all our hills. Sarah's back
at Saint Dymphna's and you can forget about

all those metaphorical storms in Oklahoma,
electric shocks are electric shocks
searing the cells of her brain.

By the time you read this letter she will have died
and risen, and died and risen again,
countless times, to who knows what new lives.

Greenbrier

We skim down over night forests,
      motor off and headlights off,
Annie and I in the truckbed
and Sarah beside you in front,
      killing another bottle of your

homemade beer—"self-medication"
      you called it today, as we painted
your ramshackle farmhouse
bright yellow to honor Van Gogh.
      And I think of the condemned

apartments the four of us once
      shared in Kentucky,
the honeycomb of doors we cut
through the walls wherever we liked,
      our lives collapsing around us

but the murals going up in every room,
      each of our countless guests
adding some token,
and all of us trusting simply in art
      until the night you sped us down

back roads to the hospital,
      my hands clamping a white T-shirt
over Sarah's wrist as she
pleaded with us to let her die.
      So now, as we coast down

to the Greenbrier River, I pick at the
       yellow paint on my hands,
study the midsummer sky.
On the riverbank, we pull off our boots
       and feel the cool

firm mud with our toes.
       One more drink, cricketsound
and whippoorwill,
and then we undress, pretending
       not to look: sheen

of white skin under black spruce,
       quick glimpses of ourselves.
Later, we drive back
slowly up the hill, then ghost
       down the other side,

drinks gone now and moon gone,
       the yellow of your place
half-hidden in shadow,
and this unexpected weariness
       when we thought we'd slipped free.

An after-midnight call from my sister
who complains that I've changed
    the poem about middle age—
        she turns forty next week, liked
the version I showed her last summer
    in which two couples, no longer young, undress

        by the Greenbrier River, think happiness
still within reach.
    Revised, the poem's couples
        still swim in the dark
waters, but are surprised, returning home,
    by their weariness.   She wants me

        to leave such sadness out, allow them
their moment of nostalgic pleasure
    without the long, moonless drive back.
        Alone now in the kitchen, I try to imagine
some parallel life for us all, see us
    emerge from the water

        at peace with our bodies.
Let some other, endlessly revised poem, detail
    the muted days and nights they shared in hospitals—
        I can't change those things—
let it suggest the struggles they'll face again
    back home.   What I want now is tall

        sedge-grass along the bank, how their clothes
unfurl into make-shift beds.
    If the rain holds off, they could stay all night.

Sarah

In the employees' bathroom, she studies
herself in the mirror, cheeks her noon dose
of lithium, fakes a swallow, then opens her mouth
wide for the imagined nurse.   Satisfied,
she flicks the pink capsule into the toilet,

strides out to the manager and quits her job,
then takes a different road home, winding
slowly above the river and the blue
weightless hills.   For the first time in months
she sings a whole symphony to herself,

this time Beethoven's 7th, both hands off the wheel
long enough to make drums thunder on the dashboard.
Finally, she stops the car, wades out singing
into tall fields.   The object has always been
to sustain song as long as possible.

Dante

She stayed up late playing set-back
    with Martin, the junkie who recites Dante
        for her in Italian, the one really

good thing, he says, he learned in the army.
    He flicked each card down
        and talked of "lucid dreaming"—knowing

you're sleeping, staying in control. Now,
    listening as steam promises more heat
        than it ever delivers, Sarah waits

for the knock and hiss of pipes to fade
    back to the dream that insisted it was real:
        she'd found a crumbling brick walkway

rescued from weeds, followed it to a ledge
    where dazzling waves rushed toward shore
        beneath her. Filled with the usual regret,

she wants to return to the dream, descend
    to the beach. Last night, she read Martin
        the label from her Salada tea bag:

"The human spirit is stronger than anything
    that can happen to it." He leaned forward, ran
        his finger gently over the long scar

on her throat, shrugged. "No one here," she said,
    "would write such crap," half-hoping
        a man who knew Dante would know what to say.

Student Art Therapist

She gives us crayons and line drawings
of Van Gogh's *Starry Night on the Rhône*

as if we could color in the spaces
he left behind.   Leaning over my page, black hair

almost brushing me, she describes how Vincent
set up his canvas by the river, four candles

burning on the brim of his hat.   I mold
bits of yellow crayon for impasto stars, want

to keep her attention, maybe touch her face, vulnerable
as any patient's . . . . She seems to notice, sways

just out of reach, still talking as loss
floods back over me.   With children's scissors

I shave ultramarine curls for the sky, then,
with my thumbs, press hard to make them stick.

The Crucifixion of the Apostle Peter

(anonymous French painting, 15th century)

Crucified upside down, eyes
    wide open, he looks out at the world
        that will survive him: kings

in the foreground, but also the detailed
    revelations of wildflowers; a town
        in the distance, rooted to the sky

by spires and towers; and swallows
    reversing their flight to catch
        dragonflies beneath harvested fields.

Say that everything he looks at
    is dying, everything already
        underground.   Nailed by his feet

he sees it rising, soldiers' scowls
    like lopsided grins, columbine
        falling in the gold hands

of ladies, each furrow of earth
    hung above heaven, and all of it,
        everything, rising, without him.

5 A.M.   The first, tired nurses slow-walk
>   the picket line, suggesting the stiff
>   Thorazine shuffle of chronic patients.   We watch
from the solarium window, loyal to our former nurses,
>   waiting for the morning's drama of hospital bus
>   nosing its way through hostile strikers.

I could watch this way in silence,
>   smoke the day into being, but my manic friend's
>   compelled to talk.   She points to the wall
of thunderclouds across the road
>   where swallows glide over blue
>   hayfields, says they shift course mid-sweep

as easily as her uncle changed subjects
>   several times in a single breath.
>   Uncle Frederic again, suggested that simply,
by the flight of birds . . . .
>   She's described him often, the favorite uncle
>   arriving with rum-filled chocolates.

This time (and why not listen?
>   the buses are late, the strikers few) it's the story
>   of Frederic's heart attack,
suffered on the road twelve hours from home.   He could have
>   stopped at a hundred hospitals
>   but wanted his family doctor.

Once, in the Cumberlands, he entered a phone booth,
  crouched ready to call for help.
     She strains her brows together, enters the story,
says he described the pain as "the devil,
    sliding her hands up under my ribs, pressing stone
fingers into my heart"—but didn't

call. The storm winds mount, the strikers
  regroup under a maple, securing their signs
    with sheets of plastic. Pinkerton guards
radio each other on the hospital grounds—yesterday
    my friend woke thinking they were soldiers.
  I try to imagine a doctor worthy of such loyalty,

picture only a man like my father, but one her uncle
  thought he knew. I light her cigarette
    from a stub of my own, urge her to finish.
She says he retold his tale so often she can see him now,
    still trying to get back
  to the point, describing blossoming orchards

caught briefly in his headlights like smoke
  over a dark lake, or the gulls that somehow
    reached the Ohio,
or his slipping past death into Indiana
    where farm buildings floated around a single
  light, and some rooster misjudged the dawn.

Prophet for the New Year

On New Year's Eve he paced the halls, urging us
to celebrate his birthday. "This is the true
Feast of the Nativity," he'd say. "Forget about Christmas,
those twenty-five fat hens lost in the snow—
that's a feast day only for wolves.
Celebrate my birthday tonight with the one
true fire—*Christus natus est!*"
All day the snow fell and he was our prophet,
the one the nurses feared.

Sometimes he spoke of the hidden years, maybe none of us
wanted to hear, but later we remembered
how his mother floated down the river
in a basket of willows—how none of the men
he ever met was his real father—and all those years
at Worcester State among the lost souls.
It was for the lost, he said,
that he had come. When he spoke of them,
he stared out the window, shook his head.

Close to midnight he came running
as if the Second Coming was at hand. "Fire!" he cried,
"Get everyone out, there's fire in here!"
The nurse tried to lead him down the hall
but the day room was transfigured
by flames. When they escorted us
to the parking lot he escaped—
we couldn't find
his footprints in the snow.

In the morning, with the snow plows, he returned.
With him he brought the good news
of the outside world:
a squad car he stole and lost in the snow—
winds that kicked up the white skirts of snow angels—
trees with inner lights.
By lunch he'd been silenced
and the first flakes of the New Year fell,
adding to the drifts that held us.

The Garden of Saint Dymphna

My roommate, perched on the window sill, tells me never
kill myself unless I make it look
accidental.   He's Catholic, thinks of others.
He's seen the Virgin Mary in the hospital garden,
standing in the ruckus of sparrows.
She wore a babushka, kept speaking in tongues,
and the half-light around her was the same
flecked gold of the Vladimir ikon.

He pointed her out in Group Therapy, but I learned
only that she had no name, that children
found her sleeping on the sidewalk off Lyndhurst Street,
and—as a joke—set her coat on fire.
I picture her waking in the night, struggling
with the burning sleeves and roaring out curses
as the children scatter.   Things aren't what I thought

they'd be.   I stick to the twelve-inch Safe Zone
along the walls, space to walk cautiously, but even here
things are never certain: the lady cop on television
recognized me this morning, pinned me with her
Stelazine-blue eyes, said, "You ruined my life.   Now,
you're gonna pay!"   He tells me never kill myself
and shows me his arms, long scars from his elbows
to his wrists, a mistake he made when he was young.

There's no privacy here.   We try to sleep but every hour
the nurse's flashlight recreates the room, then erases it.
When the children set my coat on fire they do not run.
They circle around to watch me writhe.   I retreat
to the day room and find a few patients smoking
in the semi-darkness like shadows in a station:
travelers without shoelaces or belts or the hope of a bus.

Not quite dawn and the nurse is trying to quiet him
but my roommate can't stop, his hands
tighten on the porcelain sink as he sings
the *Salve Regina* in the men's room.
The nurse calls for help but we're all
powerless, standing there in the steamed mirror
as he cries more loudly on the Mother of God.
His medicines have dried his throat and his voice cracks.

Part III

Annus Mirabilis

I unwrap two decades of David's Christmas gifts:
miniature brick fireplace, four stockings hung

from the mantel; doll's house easy chair;
and then the children—intricate carvings

of Jack and Doug, "the little boys"; a small
me, age six, still in pajamas; my sister, Joan,

white cat in her arms; and David, the oldest,
sitting on a red stool, chin in hand, gazing

intently at anything I put before him.
An entire living room—*our* room, from Maxwell Lane—

recreated, piece by piece, from David's
memory.   I remember the sofa larger,

my father's chair a darker green, but this version
of my childhood becomes each year

more the way things really were.   I unwrap
the tiny calendar, 1956, opened forever

to December, above the dates a painting
of our snowbound house.   In the nearly twenty years

his gifts have been arriving, I've seen David
only once, briefly, in San Francisco, where he told me

not to visit again.   Each year now, I recycle
my memory of his walk-up room on Mission Street,

brick and board bookcases to the ceiling, a cat
hiding somewhere in the clutter, unused to visitors.

I asked him, then, about the gifts,
what special meaning 1956 had for him,

and he shook his head, called it the *"Annus Mirabilis,"*
his eyes watering as if I, too, knew why.

I assemble the figures like characters in a crèche,
place David in a corner where he can see

the whole room.   Only in that year of miracles
are his carved brothers and sister allowed to face him.

Breaking and Entering

Strangers show me through Woodbourne.   Are they
the ones who owned this rambling house years ago
when I jimmied the kitchen window?   They serve
mint tea, show me the world map my Grandmother Minot
painted in the upstairs hall—the same map
I found on my own at sixteen, climbing
the dark stairs, wearing around my shoulders
a wool blanket from a cedar chest.
                                        I stood
at the dormer window, watching the thin
spatter of snow and the last boats of the season
swing on their moorings, halyards
chiming in an offshore wind.   Along the jetty,
one hunched gull per rock faced west.
A grown man, free to confess what a younger self
had done, I consider telling my hosts
but I'm enjoying this second tour, fear
I might spoil it.
                        That was the year I left home,
not running away I told my parents later,
just traveling.   Mother says a century ago
I'd have gone to sea.   I left Bloomington
but hitched to New England, broke
into her childhood.   I study the world
laid out in Grandmother's pastels,
her flowing calligraphy naming points of reference:
Brewster, where she was born; Buzzards Bay, outside
this window; the Sargasso Sea.
                                        I want
my hosts to leave, want this room as it was

then, frigid and littered with flies
but private.   Outside, I want that confusion
of sun, snow and orchid clouds above the estuary
where Mother fished with her father.

                              Before sunrise
she held the kerosene torch over the gunwales,
attracted eels for him to spear.   She sat
with her feet tucked under her so the slick catch
couldn't wrap around her legs.   At home her father
girdled each eel below its head, peeled
with pliers the stubborn gloves of oily skin
from white flesh.

                        Not here nor in any other memory
before she's twelve can she remember her mother.
Only after her father's death can she picture a woman
slicing something white with a fish knife, light
slanting gold through the window, then amber
through the open decanter of sherry.
It must have been about the same time
her mother painted on the wall upstairs,
mapped things out for the children or herself,
noted Buzzards Bay with a special flourish,
the "Z"s tailing recklessly to sea.

Immigrant Wife

He lures her from her skin and then hides it,
like in the stories, so she can never go back home.
He makes her learn English and bear him children, insists
that she sing to them in his tongue.   And yet,

even in English, the dark vowels of her songs
echo in the children's ears like the voice in a shell
heard miles from sea.   She folds them into beds of waves
and whispers her curse on the land.   Sometimes

the children wake to a gale of Irish and the sound
of the man roaring back at the sea.   And once, they wake
to the thin line of sunrise she traces in her wrist,
the still waters of her bath clouding like poppies.

She does not die.   She lives to be rock hard, the bitter
old Yankee who buys the house above the lake, but still,
near dawn, she dreams she might slip down to the black rocks
and swim in the skin her husband left behind at his death.

The Blasket Clearances

(an American woman at Dunquin)

Too blustery today to cross to the island
so I drink sloe gin in the guest house, unwrap
the framed photograph I bought in Dingle—
the last boat leaving the Blaskets, 1953.
Seven men kneel in a curragh, four of them

looking up at the camera, their numb faces
awash in the same light that dazzles waves and headland.
My father left in such a boat, a few years before this,
always with his sense of when to get out.
But then he's in Worcester,

quarreling with Mother while I watch
from the neighbor's door
as he throws drawer after drawer
of our clothing down the sleet-glazed ravine.
But he doesn't leave for good.   He goes

back to work for the Highway, appears next day
with a newspaper-cone filled with roses.
Mother hesitates so I run to him,
take him back, am lifted into the air and then sandwiched
in a cautious, three-person hug.

Earlier this July afternoon I wore my thick, wool coat
as I walked in gale winds around Slea Head.   I kept
peering out at the island, guessing which fleck of white
was once his cottage, judged him for leaving.
What would it have taken to hold him?

Another glass of gin.   Studying the photograph
where strong men leave home on a sunny day, I shiver
as if he were looking over my shoulder from some
near-by purgatory for lapsed Catholics . . . .
I'll never accept Mother's reasons

for his leaving, or the unasked-for prayers of that
fucking priest in the hospital
when Father turned up, comatose, in Springfield.
He left, then, as he'd left
six years before, by the back door, without goodbyes.

Again, the sun-lit faces of men leaving the island:
weary, resigned, emptied at last of all feeling.   It's not
that I ever needed reasons, it's just
that in the hospital the same sun kept shifting
on his forehead, light playing above the undertow.

Houses in Cézanne

Her first lesson: he wouldn't even let her touch
the keyboard.   He had her drum fingers

against a table, work the stone from her wrists.
We all start with stone.   Now, she plays Satie

on the museum bench, stares up at houses
in Cézanne.   Peeled and cubed like fresh-cut potatoes

the homes recall her jumbled village,
before the tanks.   The house on the right

might be her family's—
she stands up, approaches, imagines her father

enthroned at his piano.   As a child
she begged for attention and got

Stravinsky.   Her father played *The Firebird* from memory
and she danced, furiously, the story

hidden in the notes: There is a magician, her father said,
who turns all travelers to stone.

If you get the chance, kill him.   If you find
the devil's egg where he hides his soul, smash it.

But when the magician appeared he stood in a jeep
surrounded by soldiers.   Her useless potato knife

hidden in her scarf, she was thrust
outside with the others to watch Reb Zalman hang.

In the climate-controlled Impressionist wing
she sits back down, gives Cézanne the distance

he seems to need.   She fingers her watch, gold
like the one her father gave a guard,

barter for her life.   From a rise she looked back
and found the houses a sift of chalk and ocher and rose

in which the soldiers, the music and her family
vanished, and only the planes

of white-washed walls gave back the sun.

Altenbrücken

In the bookstalls along the river, I find
the girl of my dreams selling old
gravestones stacked in wood bins, white
marble inscribed in Gothic script and smooth
slate markers, the names forgotten.
I sort them out, my grandparents and great-
grandparents, and count the generations,
one stone upon the next.   Taking my hands, she
teaches me to deal the stones like Tarot cards,
shows me how they point towards dusk.

That night I dance with her
outside the Hotel Hölderlin beneath
chestnut trees and Chinese lanterns.
We waltz among gaily dressed couples
who draw no breath—sometimes
they stop to stare at me, wondering
that the living come so close.
Later, beneath the old bridge, she
offers me the mist rising as the river
breathes.   Passing through her lips

I find myself in a small room, playing violin
for those who have ears, bringing them
gifts from the dead.   For those who weep:
spirited dances.   For those who laugh:
Trauermusik, so in the strain of the bow
they hear their passing.   I shape the notes
this woman gives me, here in her bed
with the river set above us like a canopy.
For a thousand years I'll be this music:
sound of water passing under stone.

Game Near Ocotal

(for Paul Graseck, Nicaragua, 1984)

Too dark to dig bomb shelters: they lay their shovels down
and walk to the ball field.   Young boys guard the foul lines,
staring up at black hills as they swing their M-16s like bats.

A man with one arm pitches out of the darkness to his son
who swings hard and misses and they all laugh: it's only a game
played out on the border where everything disappears

sooner or later, but when a batter makes contact he roars down
imaginary baselines, taking the shortstop out with a high slide
or tearing blindly for home, head down and furious.

Chandeliers in the Desert

In Las Vegas, we felt like kids—were
kids, posing as gamblers at the casinos.
They said come back when we were twenty-one,
       showed us slot machines in the lobby.
       I don't remember winning ever, but Seth, annoying

the attendant with his Bogart imitations,
had a brief run.   I settled for Dostoevsky, losing
gloriously, thinking I knew at last
       why he pawned his wife's rings, this prolonged swoon
       of loss sustained under brilliant chandeliers.

This was not, I thought then, what we'd come for,
why we rushed cross-country and Seth,
to keep me awake so we'd make good time,
       read *The Brothers Karamazov* out loud.
       He couldn't drive—a surprising flaw

for a boy who took college classes and smoked—
so chapters and landscapes merged: even now,
the Grand Inquisitor rules the plains
       approaching Denver.
                          One evening, the desert road
       stretched out before us, I gave Seth the wheel.

Leaning back, baffled I hadn't tried this earlier,
I watched the operatic night come on, and then—
the Volkswagen shuddering beneath me—woke
       afraid I was sleeping at the wheel.   Seth sang
       with the radio, pointed to the red needle trembling

near ninety, the fastest, he said, my car could go.
He gestured grandly to the empty road,
said, "In the desert, all is permitted."
         We didn't finish Dostoevsky for another year,
         and then, separately, miles apart.

Seth wrote postcards from Prague, then Istanbul,
made up wild stories that, who knows,
maybe were true.   There's a snapshot of us
         leaning against the rusted fenders
         of the '62 Beetle we named Grushenka.

A road sign—it should have been neon—
welcomes us to Vegas.   We're side by side,
grinning at the camera, but Seth's
         troubled eyebrows distort his smile, the same
         smile he wore when, unable to slow him down

I slumped back, tried to enjoy the world
lunging towards me, the way it blurred
and shook until the desert sky was alive,
         points of light convulsing above us
         as we hit ninety.

Abington Four-Corners

An open-and-shut day, sun skittering
through clouds, and I linger in bed, look through
old journals, this time the Bohemian Forest, 1969.
In the train station at Železná Ruda
a girl with waist-long hair sits
by a wood-burning stove, sells me my ticket.
We're alone in this remote station,
it's early morning, and though we do no more
than talk a bit in the German she finds
painful to use, I take with me the impression of dark
smoke-scented hair.   On this trip I'm reading,
with help from a German dictionary,
Nietzsche's *Birth of Tragedy,* see everything
as Apollonian or Dionysian,
especially the black steam-engine
carrying a red star through the forests
to Prague.
       Then there's the "party
for the American," thrown by a new friend,
the Czech drama student who helped
talk me down from a bad trip.   I'm grateful,
now, to that eighteen-year-old I once was,
crouching in the rain on my friend's
red-tile roof, that he did not jump,
that he clung to the possible recovery
of his world.
       Anne comes, returns me
to the present with a mug of espresso,
points out the sparkling orioles' nest slung
from a branch of our dying maple: tinsel
from some past Christmas, woven

with twigs and baling twine
into an odd assemblage of the humble and gaudy.
I read her the passage that now seems
almost comic, my Czech friend on the roof
coaxing me down with Rilke.
"Jeder Engel ist schrecklich," he admits,
"and yet Rilke sings to these angels,
Rilke lives with these angels."
I stagger back down to the window,
not wanting to hear about Rilke, needing
only the ordinary things I fear I've lost.
Anne finds none of this
funny, and I guess I agree.
                    I'm balancing
my coffee on one knee, watching her dress
in the sunny room, searching for the word—
nimbus?—to describe the shimmer on her skin.
Open-and-shut day: her phrase, the gloomy clouds
and moments of light that leave me, happily,
half-blind.   I put the coffee aside, try
to convince her I'm a luminous cloud
with huge *sfumato* hands, gentle as a god.
But my timing's off, the sun's gone,
and she's troubled, besides, at the many ways
I've almost killed myself.
                    Back in bed, I try
to salvage the mood by skipping ahead to Vienna
where we're reunited, the little room
on the Gürtel, and the Brueghels
in the Kunsthistorische Museum, my answer

to all that business about Nietszche.
See, these sketches I made of a wedding feast,
inhabitants of that world I thought I'd lost:
revelers in a village dance (a few
about to quarrel) or this triangle of hunters
trudging with their twelve tired dogs
through snow, a lone fox hung from a staff,
and below them some Flemish village,
clearly their home, where peasants skate
on flooded fields.   Isn't this a beauty
neither Apollonian nor Dionysian
but simply earthly?   Granted
a place where tragedy's never far off—here's
a family in the distance, fighting a chimney fire—
but still, a place where burnished light
with its perfect timing floods our room again.

Gloria

The photograph in this morning's *Chronicle*
shows the steeple of Willimantic's Congregational Church
toppling in the '38 Hurricane, a shot that means

someone stood on Valley Street during the storm's height,
captured the exact moment the spire buckled
over its tower, poised above an elm also gone now.

Imagine that unidentified photographer, shielding the lens
with his hand, waiting on the deserted street for—what?
the steeple's fall? or the power hidden in this world

to manifest itself, an act of God we say
because like God we think we cannot know ourselves
without it.   Three years ago

patients slept in beds we'd pulled to the hall
the night Gloria approached.   As wind battered glass
I played gin with a pianist from East Hartford—

we might have been old friends, sitting up late
in some all-night cafe, though I was the one
that day who found his hidden syringe.

Watching from the wire-and-glass window, we worried
for our families, but when I pointed out the snow plows
brought to clear September roads of pine boughs and debris—

those blue sparks the steel plow struck from blacktop—
he sensed my love of storms, turned to me, half-smiling,
asked how much damage it would take to really satisfy me.

Hurricane's Edge

I swam sidestroke so I could watch
as you vanished behind each wave,

then reappeared and vanished again—
the most vivid memory of my childhood

a half-blind, rain-blurred vision of you rising
and falling as wind tore spume

off the crests of waves.
Strange though, recalling this

I see you as you are now, at sixty,
remember all of it so clearly

except your face, as it was then . . . .
I start over, see us board

the windows of the beach house
we'd been warned to leave,

recall that feeling of almost-
safety, all our necessities

laid out around us.
And then you open the door to the storm

and I follow, stumbling through frenzied eelgrass.
I think we will turn back at the brown waves

but you wade in and start to swim.
Mother, I see a nine-year-old

searching for you, see myself treading in place,
rising over a crest and then—yes—

a glimpse of you, almost sheltered
in the trough of a wave, young again,

turning back to look for me:
in your face a terrifying joy.

Theodore Robert Lynn Deppe was born in Duluth, Minnesota, in 1950, and grew up in Indiana. He holds a B.A. in English from Earlham College, a B.S. in Nursing from Berea College, and an M.F.A. in Writing from Vermont College. His work has appeared in a chapbook, *Necessary Journeys*, and in many journals, and he has received a grant from the Connecticut Commission on the Arts. He lives in Abington, Connecticut, with his wife and three children.

POETRY FROM ALICE JAMES BOOKS

The Calling   Tom Absher
Thirsty Day   Kathleen Aguero
In the Mother Tongue   Catherine Anderson
Personal Effects   Becker, Minton, Zuckerman
Backtalk   Robin Becker
Legacies   Suzanne E. Berger
Disciplining the Devil's Country   Carole Borges
Afterwards   Patricia Cumming
Letter from an Outlying Province   Patricia Cumming
Riding with the Fireworks   Ann Darr
Chemo-Poet and Other Poems   Helene Davis
Children of the Air   Theodore Deppe
ThreeSome Poems,   Dobbs, Gensler, Knies
The Forked Rivers   Nancy Donegan
33   Marjorie Fletcher
US: Women   Marjorie Fletcher
No One Took a Country from Me   Jacqueline Frank
Forms of Conversion   Allison Funk
Natural Affinities   Erica Funkhouser
Rush to the Lake   Forrest Gander
Without Roof   Kinereth Gensler
Bonfire   Celia Gilbert
Permanent Wave   Miriam Goodman
Signal::Noise   Miriam Goodman
Romance and Capitalism at the Movies   Joan Joffe Hall
Raw Honey   Marie Harris
Making the House Fall Down   Beatrice Hawley
The Old Chore   John Hildebidle
Impossible Dreams   Pati Hill
Robeson Street   Fanny Howe
The Chicago Home   Linnea Johnson
From Room to Room   Jane Kenyon
Streets after Rain   Elizabeth Knies
Sleep Handbook   Nancy Lagomarsino

Dreaming in Color   Ruth Lepson
Falling Off the Roof   Karen Lindsey
Temper   Margo Lockwood
Black Dog   Margo Lockwood
Rosetree   Sabra Loomis
Shrunken Planets   Robert Louthan
Animals   Alice Mattison
The Common Life   David McKain
The Canal Bed   Helena Minton
Your Skin Is a Country   Nora Mitchell
Openers   Nina Nyhart
French for Soldiers   Nina Nyhart
Night Watches: Inventions on the Life of Maria Mitchell   Carole Oles
Wolf Moon   Jean Pedrick
Pride & Splendor   Jean Pedrick
The Hardness Scale   Joyce Peseroff
Before We Were Born   Carol Potter
Lines Out   Rosamund Rosenmeier
The Country Changes   Lee Rudolph
Curses   Lee Rudolph
Box Poems   Willa Schneberg
Against That Time   Ron Schreiber
Moving to a New Place   Ron Schreiber
Contending with the Dark   Jeffrey Schwartz
Changing Faces   Betsy Sholl
Appalachian Winter   Betsy Sholl
Rooms Overhead   Betsy Sholl
From This Distance   Susan Snively
Deception Pass   Sue Standing
Blue Holes   Laurel Trivelpiece
Home.Deep.Blue New and Selected Poems   Jean Valentine
The Trans-Siberian Railway   Cornelia Veenendaal
Green Shaded Lamps   Cornelia Veenendaal
Old Sheets   Larkin Warren
Tamsen Donner: a woman's journey   Ruth Whitman
Permanent Address   Ruth Whitman